THE OFFICIAL  RSPCA PET GUIDE

Care for your

Goldfis

CW00385667

Tina Hearne

Contents

Acknowledgements

Heather Angel, John Clegg, Eric Hosking, Laurence Perkins, Spectrum

Illustrations by Dietrich Burkel, Baz East

First published 1980
Third reprint 1983
Revised edition 1985
9 8 7 6 5 4 3 2 1

Published by William Collins Sons and Company Limited
London · Glasgow · Sydney · Auckland · Toronto · Johannesburg
© Royal Society for the Prevention of Cruelty to Animals 1980
Printed in Italy by New Interlitho, Milan

ISBN 0 00 410221 5

Collins

Record Card

Record sheet for your own goldfish

Name

Date of birth
(actual or estimated)

Variety   Sex

Colour/description

photograph or portrait

Feeding notes

Medical record

Growth record

Breeding record
(if applicable)

Veterinary surgeon's name

Surgery hours

Practice address

Tel. no.

Choosing a Goldfish

The goldfish, first bred by the Chinese a thousand years ago, and introduced into Britain in the early eighteenth century, remains the most popular of the coldwater fish that can be kept in captivity.

Since fish are dependent on dissolved oxygen for their breathing, it is perhaps surprising that any can survive captivity for long. It is possible only because certain of them, notably the rather sluggish bottom-feeders, such as Tench, can survive on far less oxygen than most. The goldfish has only a very modest oxygen requirement, usually satisfied in a garden pond, or in a well maintained aquarium. Goldfish bowls, such as that illustrated, are too limited to be satisfactory. Their oxygen is so rapidly depleted that, for this reason alone, they are unsuitable.

It often happens that goldfish are won at fêtes and fairs, and so introduced to a family with no time for preparation. The practice of giving away live animals as prizes is not illegal, however distasteful it may be, but the mortality rate among such goldfish is high.

In an attempt to be responsible, stallholders often give the prize winners a small screw of paper containing enough fish food for the weekend, but it is unlikely fish would die of starvation in 48 hours. It is suffocation, or a sudden temperature fluctuation that can kill.

Those who accept goldfish as prizes should control their natural impulse to tip the fish directly from its plastic bag into a bowl of cold water. It is far safer to float the opened bag in the bowl until the water temperatures correspond. Goldfish can accept a big range of temperatures, if they have time to accommodate to it slowly. A sudden change of only 1°C/2°F may be fatal.

Fortunately, most goldfish keepers, deciding for themselves when they want to buy stock, will have the time to make adequate preparation. Happily, it seems there is always room for a pond, even in the smallest garden; and space for an aquarium, even in the most restricted accommodation.

Unsuitable accommodation: bad points include restricted space even for solitary fish; lack of shade and privacy; small surface area resulting in poor oxygenation; curved sides that cause water to heat up and lose oxygen

Biology

Lateral line   The lateral line is a major sense organ common to all fish. It is a line of specialized cells forming a fluid-filled canal, which makes the fish highly sensitive to the smallest disturbance of the water. Even very slight movement in the water will set up vibrations in this canal, so alerting the goldfish to obstacles and to danger.

Eyes   The bulbous eyes of the Telescopic-eyed Moor have been exaggerated by selective breeding, but all goldfish have slightly protuberant eyes. These compensate for their not being able to turn the head. The result is a very wide field of vision, effectively enabling the fish to see all round.

The eyes are entirely unprotected, with no eyelids. This is not a disadvantage to goldfish kept in a pond, but those in aquaria need to be shaded from direct sunshine.

Telescopic-eyed Black Moor

Gills   All fish breathe by means of gills. These are internal organs where the exchange of gases takes place as a current of water is circulated through them. Dissolved oxygen from the water passes into the blood, carbon dioxide from the blood passes into the water. The water enters by way of the mouth, passes through the gills and out by way of the gill covers or opercula.

Temperature   Goldfish are cold-blooded, or poikilothermic. Their body temperature is not stable, but fluctuates with the water temperature. Goldfish are able to tolerate the big range of temperature they experience at different times of year in a garden pool because the variation is gradual. A sudden change of temperature, even if small, can be fatal. This is probably a significant factor in the high mortality rate of goldfish kept in captivity.

Gill cover

Pectoral fin

Pelvic or Ventral fin

Paired fins   The paired pectoral fins, just behind the gill opening, correspond to the fore limbs of land vertebrates. Their particular function is to act as brakes. A swimming goldfish will brake by extending both pectoral fins simultaneously. When extended, the drag they exert on the forward motion is sufficient to stop the fish. These fins are also used by the fish to change direction. By extending one, so that the drag is exerted on that side only, the fish can swing itself round to reverse its direction completely.

The paired pelvic fins correspond to the hind limbs of land vertebrates. To a lesser extent,

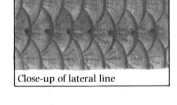

Close-up of lateral line

these too are used in braking, but their particular function is to stabilize the fish by correcting the lift that occurs when the pectorals are used. Both sets of paired fins work like this, as hydroplanes, to control the rise and fall of the fish in the water.

Median fins The dorsal and anal fins are known, because of their position, as the median fins. Their structure is common to all the fins. Essentially they are folds of skin stretched over a light framework of fin rays. They are so fine that, in their median position, they are able to cut through the water with very little resistance, although some fast-swimming fish are able to fold down the dorsal fin when swimming at speed. The function of the median fins is to act as keels. By greatly increasing the longitudinal surface of the fish, they are able to give stability by preventing yawing and rolling.

Scales The scales are thin, bony plates, overlapped from the head towards the tail for minimal resistance to the water, which form a complete, protective body covering. Each lays down extra growth rings with age, which can be seen under a microscope and interpreted by an experienced scale-reader.

Single scale

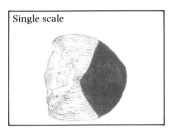

Backbone The goldfish is a vertebrate, with a highly developed nervous system, and as such is protected by law, with all other captive vertebrates.

The backbone is very flexible, adapted to bear the strain of the constant, sinuous movements of swimming. Spines, corresponding to the rib bones of land vertebrates, are attached to the backbone, but they do not form a rib cage for the major organs. Instead these are contained in a membranous sac suspended from the backbone.

Cutaway to show backbone

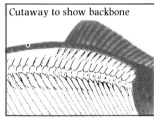

Dorsal fin

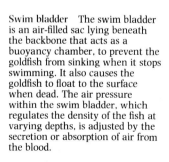

Caudal fin

Anal fin

Vent

Caudal fin The caudal, or tail fin, is used to help propel the fish through the water. The movements of the caudal fin are generated by the alternate contraction of strong muscles lying on each side of the backbone. These muscles cause the sinuous swimming movement that passes, like waves, down the length of the body from head to tail.

Selective breeding from mutant forms has produced certain varieties of fancy goldfish, like this Comet, with vastly exaggerated tail fin.

Swim bladder The swim bladder is an air-filled sac lying beneath the backbone that acts as a buoyancy chamber, to prevent the goldfish from sinking when it stops swimming. It also causes the goldfish to float to the surface when dead. The air pressure within the swim bladder, which regulates the density of the fish at varying depths, is adjusted by the secretion or absorption of air from the blood.

Comet

Fancy Varieties

It is possible to choose from some one hundred fancy varieties which have been bred from mutants of the Common goldfish. The fancy varieties show great divergence of body shape, fins, eyes, colour and scales. In general they are smaller, less hardy than the Common goldfish and shorter lived.

The Comet
The nearest in form to the Common goldfish, the Comet, has a more streamlined body and an exaggerated caudal fin that accounts for half its length. One of the hardiest of the fancy varieties, the Comet may be kept out in a garden pond all year and may live to approximately 14 years, for the Comet is also the longest lived of all the fancy varieties of goldfish.

The Shubunkins
The Shubunkins are renowned for their incredible blue colour, mottled with black, red, brown, yellow and violet. There are two varieties: the London, which retains the outline of the Common goldfish, and the Bristol, which has the outline of the Comet. The London, being the hardier of the two, may be kept in a pond all year; the Bristol should be brought in for the winter and kept in a tank.

Sarasa Comet Goldfish

Bristol Shubunkin

The Fantail
The Fantail has a spherical body, well-developed fins and a deeply forked tail. There are two types: a 'visibly scaled' variety with the normal gold colouring, and a 'calico' variety with the colouring of the Shubunkins, which is due to an absence of pigment under the scales. Only the scaled Fantail is hardy.

The Veiltail
Another spherical variety, with the most excessive fin development, this has a divided caudal fin that hangs in folds. Because of possible damage to the fins, the Veiltails are most usually kept in aquaria. Visibly scaled and calico varieties are bred.

The Black Moor
Sometimes called the Telescopic-eyed Moor, this is a fish with the outline of the Veiltail, and should always be kept in an aquarium to safeguard the fins and protuberant eyes. Show specimens are entirely black.

The Lionhead and Oranda
Two bizarre fish, most suitable for aquaria, each with the appearance of having a mane. Scaled or calico.

Veiltail Goldfish

Adult Oranda showing typical head development

The Common Goldfish

Despite the tempting diversity found among the fancy varieties, the Common goldfish, with its purity of line and extravagant colour, remains one of the most beautiful of all fish. The strong red-gold colour is always associated with the name, but many specimens are yellow-gold, and others show patches of silver or black.

For the novice fish keeper, the Common goldfish is the most suitable choice. The fancy varieties have, in some respects, been weakened by selective breeding which has to concentrate on certain characteristics of form and colour; the Common goldfish retains the remarkable hardiness of the species.

Until they measure 12.5cm/5in the Common goldfish are suitable for keeping in an aquarium, together with similarly sized fish of the Comet, London Shubunkin and visibly scaled Fantail varieties. Over this size, all these would be too confined in a tank. They need the freedom of a pond, which they are hardy enough to tolerate all year round in Britain.

In five years, the Common goldfish may have reached a length of 20cm/8in in favourable conditions; some eventually attain 40cm/16in in length and an age of some 25 years.

Common Goldfish and Lionhead
When calculating the fish capacity of a tank estimate length of fish *without* the tailfin

Aquaria

Fish capacity of tanks
Tanks of various construction and price are available, but size and surface area are the most important considerations. The smallest practicable tank would measure 45 × 30 × 30cm/18 × 12 × 12in, holding 40l/9gal; a much better size would be 60 × 38 × 30cm/24 × 15 × 12in, holding 72l/15gal.

To calculate how many small fish may be kept in a tank safely, two rules of thumb apply. Either allow 2.5cm/1in of fish to 4.5l/1gal of water; or 60sq cm/24sq in of surface to 2.5cm/1in of fish. Of the two, the latter is the more important, because an adequate surface area allows for good oxygenation.

Aeration
The fish capacity of a tank is greatly increased by aeration, perhaps by as much as 40%, but it is not necessary to aerate a tank for coldwater fish unless there is a danger of overcrowding.

Heating and lighting
Goldfish need to be kept within the limits $10° - 21°C/50° - 70°F$, which are likely to be met in most living rooms in Britain throughout the year, without the use of an aquarium heater.

Artificial lighting is usually unnecessary for the goldfish, although the aquarium plants will thrive best with 8–10 hours of top lighting a day.

Position
For preference, the aquarium should be kept in a good north light, but not on a window sill where it may be subjected to extremes of temperature.

It is important that the tank be protected from direct sunlight which overheats the water, causing it to hold less oxygen in solution, encourages the growth of algae and is too strong for the unprotected eyes of the goldfish (p 8).

Fish capacity of tank   To calculate how many fish may safely be kept in a tank, allow 60sq cm/24sq in of surface area for every centimetre/inch of fish, estimated without including the tail fin. The tank should be understocked to begin with, to allow for the growth of the fish

Surface area   Any fish tank needs a large surface area for good oxygenation of the water. A tall, narrow tank may hold an equivalent amount of water, but the restricted surface area would greatly reduce its 'fish capacity', which is the number of fish that may be kept in the tank safely

Pondweeds   A selection of submerged pondweeds (p. 19) will provide both food and shade, besides enhancing the look of the aquarium

Shelter   The fish need shade from bright sunlight, and sheltering places. Hiding places can be provided by using rounded stones to form caves. Sharp-edged stones, or decorations such as sea urchins are potentially dangerous to the fish, who are liable to damage scales on them

Ventilated cover   A ventilated cover will serve to keep dust off the surface of the water, allowing for better oxygenation of the water. It will also keep the fish safe from cats, and from jumping out of the tank in fright at a sudden disturbance

Feeding ring   Goldfish will feed according to the temperature: probably twice a day in summer; once in winter. The use of a feeding ring prevents food floating over the surface of the tank, and makes for easier cleaning

Paper frieze   A paper frieze, fixed to the back of the tank, will filter bright sunlight in summer, making the tank more comfortable for the fish, and controlling the summer growth of algae

Tank maintenance   Aquarists sell scrapers for removing algae from the glass sides of the tank, and suction cleaners for siphoning off detritus, or decaying matter, from the base gravel

A Garden Pond

Depth of water
If the garden pond is to be suitable for fish all year round, the water will need to be 38–45cm/15–18in deep overall, with a shallow margin of 15cm/6in where it will quickly warm up on an early summer day to encourage spawning. When, in severe weather, the surface water begins to ice over, the fish will congregate in the deepest part of the pond. Shallow ponds, which are subject to rapid fluctuations of temperature and are liable to freeze solid at times, should be used only as temporary summer ponds.

Excavation
When excavating for a pool, these depths should be taken into account, making allowance for the fact that the water level will be lower than ground level. The area of the pond needs to be big enough for its fringes to be planted with the rhizomes of water plants such as yellow flag (p 18), which need room to spread.

Once excavated, the area should be lined with sifted soil, sand or newspapers, which act as underlay for the pool liner. Without this, it is possible for the pool to be punctured by stones.

Pool liners
Of the many pool liners available, heavy duty black polythene is effective and inexpensive, but only short-lived. Reinforced PVC or butyl are much more substantial and have the advantage that, once damaged, they can be patched. Pre-formed fibreglass pool liners are excellent, but must be big enough to give good shelter in winter.

Situation
Ponds are best sited away from overhanging trees. Falling leaves soon choke a pond, and unless raked out, will deplete the oxygen level in the water as they decompose. If leaves are unavoidable, then the pond may be netted in autumn while they are falling.

Choosing fish

Suitable fish for a garden pond all year are the Common goldfish, Comet, London Shubunkin and visibly scaled Fantail, particularly larger specimens.

During the summer only, certain of the less hardy fancy varieties will be safe in the pond, including the Bristol Shubunkin and calico Fantail.

Compatible species for the pond are Tench, useful as bottom feeders, which scavenge food wasted by the surface feeders; Golden Rudd, again bottom feeders, but active and showy enough for their bright red fins to give a welcome flash of colour; and Golden Orfe, beautiful surface feeders, nearly always in sight.

Polythene-lined garden pond

Goldfish pond　The goldfish pond is the ideal accommodation for all hardy goldfish (p. 13). There is room enough here for a small shoal of fish to live together, with adequate shade, shelter, depth of water, and natural food

Inset　The inset shows how a shallow marginal area can be constructed easily, with soil retained behind a low line of bricks. Without a shallow margin, emergent plants such as flags will need to be grown in baskets, as water-lilies

Icing　Hardy goldfish (p. 13) may safely be left in a garden pond all winter, providing the overall depth *of water* is approximately 45cm/ 18in. In cold weather the fish will congregate at the bottom of the pond where they will remain unfrozen, albeit in a sluggish state.

　Smashing the ice may lead to fish fatalities, due to shock, but it is sometimes possible to open up small air-holes at the surface by floating balls on the pond at night, and removing them during the day when temperatures may rise above freezing.

　Siphoning off a few inches of water beneath the ice will leave space for a layer of air, allowing oxygen to be dissolved in the water to replenish supplies

Fountain   Even in a pond there may sometimes be a shortage of oxygen, for instance in hot weather. A fountain or hose-pipe played on the pond at a critical time, as when fish are seen to gulp at the surface, will aerate the water temporarily

Autumn leaves   It is advisable to net the pond in autumn, to catch falling leaves that will otherwise choke the pond and use up its oxygen during decomposition. If trapped under ice, fish may suffer serious oxygen starvation if there are decaying leaves depleting the oxygen level

Lawn surround   A lawn surround, likely to drain into the pond, should never be treated with chemicals such as weed-killers, that may also kill the fish

Water-lilies   Water-lilies can be positioned in planting baskets anywhere in the pond. They provide valuable shade and shelter for the fish, but may need lifting and pruning annually in favourable conditions, to limit growth

Floating plants   Floating plants, such as *Azolla*, provide shade, shelter, and food for the fish. They also inhibit the growth of algae in summer, by shading the surface

Red Lionhead Veiltail Goldfish

Common Goldfish

Telescopic-Eyed Goldfish

ancy Goldfish including Orandas, Bubble-Eye and juvenile Red-Capped Lionhead

Fantails

Water Plants

The emergent plants
(suitable for ponds)
These are the marginal plants, such as arrow-head, marsh marigold, bulrush, water forget-me-not and yellow flag, which in nature grow at the water's edge, with roots submerged and the leaves and flowers emerging above the surface. Besides adding to the beauty of the pond, the emergent plants, growing in a shallow margin, provide a spawning place for the adult goldfish and also some shelter for the young fry.

They can be planted in an artificial pond using a low wall to retain the soil, as shown on p 14, or in planting baskets. However, they all have stout, creeping rhizomes that need cutting back annually in favourable situations where they can become very invasive.

Floating-leaved plants
(suitable for ponds)
Like the emergent plants, the best known of the floating-leaved plants, the water lily, has thick rhizomes that may also silt up the pond unless cut back when necessary. A specialist nursery will supply water lilies in planting baskets suitable for use in an artificial pond. As varieties of water lily grow to different heights, care must be taken to position the baskets at the correct depth so that the leaves will all lie on the surface.

Apart from their spectacular beauty, the water lilies, and the other well-known floating-leaved plant, the water crowfoot, provide sheltered resting places for the fish, and by shading the surface, inhibit the growth of algae.

Floating plants
(for ponds and aquaria)
These are small water plants which float freely on the surface, trailing fine, aquatic roots. The best known are duckweed and frogbit, which are able to take nutrients directly from the water by means of their roots.

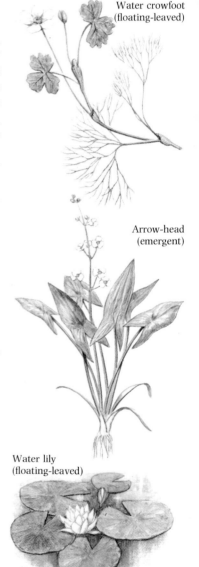

Water crowfoot
(floating-leaved)

Arrow-head
(emergent)

Water lily
(floating-leaved)

Hornwort
(submerged)

Canadian pondweed
(submerged)

Water milfoil (submerged)

Curly pondweed
(submerged)

Azolla
(floating)

Although these plants provide food and shelter for the goldfish and inhibit the growth of algae, they multiply fast and can eventually cover the whole surface. For this reason, it may be better to introduce the less hardy *Azolla* or *Salvinia*. These are sub-tropical species which may possibly fail to over-winter in Britain, but they are the most suitable floating plants for an aquarium.

Submerged plants
(for ponds and aquaria)

These are the plants usually referred to as water weeds. They include Canadian pondweed, curly pondweed, eel grass, hornwort and water milfoil. These plants grow submerged and are particularly suited to aquaria where their beauty of form is best displayed.

Submerged plants feed through their stems and their finely divided or ribbon-shaped leaves. Their roots can be anchored in the gravel, perhaps weighted by a stone or a small lead strip.

These are the plants said to be valuable in aquaria as oxygenators, since they give off oxygen in daytime during their feeding process of photosynthesis. They also use up oxygen throughout the 24 hours for respiration and a heavily planted aquarium can be deficient in oxygen at night.

Even so, the plants are valuable because they can absorb carbon dioxide and grow on the waste products found in any aquarium as the detritus – the debris – on the floor of the aquarium decomposes. This has the effect of cleaning the tank.

Submerged plants also provide shade and food for the fish. Goldfish will eat the green plants directly, and also the minute organisms that are always found attached to these, as to all water plants.

The most vigorous plants will need some pruning, and small bundles of cuttings will root if anchored into the gravel at the base of an aquarium tank.

Feeding

Temperature

The rate at which goldfish feed is determined, like all their activity, by the temperature of their surroundings, on which, as cold blooded animals, they are totally dependent. Goldfish feed best at 16°–18°C/62°–68°F. Outside the range 10°–21°C/50°–70°F they are too inactive to feed, either because of cold or because warmer water is deficient in oxygen.

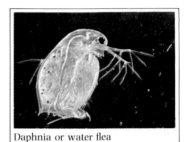
Daphnia or water flea

Quantity of food

At a temperature of 16°–18°C/62°–68°F, goldfish feed so well they will probably need two meals a day, whereas when sluggish, one meal a day, or even one meal every other day is sufficient.

Each meal should be eaten in ten minutes and the amount adjusted accordingly. Uneaten food just sinks to the bottom, and decays with the other detritus, using up oxygen in the process and fouling the water.

Healthy fish can last two or three weeks without food, for instance, during a family holiday but must be in clean water, preferably with water plants.

Freshwater shrimp

Goldfish food

In a well-stocked garden pond, goldfish have a natural, mixed diet of green plants, aquatic insects and, perhaps, very small fish. This can be supplemented, if necessary, with proprietary fish food.

In an aquarium, the fish can be kept on a high protein dried fish food, supplemented with water plants or a little chopped lettuce, and water fleas, freshwater shrimps and lice and *Tubifex* worms, all of which are available as a frozen diet.

Water lice or water slaters

Feeding ring

The use of a feeding ring is recommended, since it controls the spread of the food in the tank and makes cleaning much easier.

Mass of *Tubifex* worms

Feeding ring on surface of water

Maintenance

Aquaria The single most important fact about maintenance is that if the water becomes cloudy it must be changed. Foul water holds very little oxygen in solution and the fish are in danger of suffocation.

Novice fish keepers, who are understandably liable to make elementary mistakes such as overfeeding, will need to change the water far more frequently than an experienced aquarist.

The danger of plunging fish directly into water freshly drawn from the mains supply is that the sudden change in temperature may be fatal and the chlorine content is harmful to fish. The procedure, therefore, is to draw off buckets of water and leave them standing all day to reach room temperature and to give time for the chlorine fumes to disperse.

Ponds Ponds will need cleaning out periodically to remove decaying vegetation and to thin out water plants. If algal growth is too vigorous to be controlled by hand weeding, all the fish and plants should be removed temporarily and the algae killed off with a dark red solution of potassium permanganate. After some three days the pond will need to be drained, rinsed, refilled and the fish and plants reintroduced. Beware of reintroducing algae when restocking.

Scraping algae

Handling

Fish are highly sensitive creatures, easily hurt by careless handling, easily shocked by sudden changes in temperature or light and by strong vibrations.

When moving fish to temporary accommodation, it is important to protect them from injury by using a net or a jug to catch them. If the hands are used, it is likely that scales will be torn off, allowing *Saprolegnia* (p 24) to enter. Once this fungus spreads to the gill covers, it can cause interference with breathing and subsequent death.

Temporary accommodation needs to be prepared long enough in advance for the temperature to be within 1°C/2°F of the permanent accommodation at that time. The shock of a sudden change of temperature greater than this is sufficient sometimes to kill.

It is also dangerous to plunge fish from sudden light into darkness, or *vice versa*. In a strip-lit aquarium, the strip should be turned off before the room lights at night to make the transition to darkness more gradual.

Fish are also shocked by sudden noise and vibration, such as tapping on the side of the tank. Fish have even died after being stranded out of water, having jumped out in fright. This is one reason for having a ventilated lid.

Scooping fish

Ailments

Oxygen starvation

Gaping at the surface is a sign of oxygen starvation. It may be due to several causes, but should be dealt with immediately.

Oxygen starvation can happen in a pond as a result of overcrowding, decomposing vegetation, shallow water, which tends to overheat on a hot day, or blanket weed choking the surface. The oxygen level of the water can quickly be improved by playing a fountain, or a hose-pipe on the surface.

In an aquarium, oxygen starvation would be due to similar causes. The immediate action is to siphon off some of the water from the bottom of the aquarium, and to replenish the tank with clean water. Subsequently it is vital to correct the basic reason for poor oxygenation, taking the advice of a professional aquarist if the reason is obscure.

White fungus disease, *Saprolegnia*

This is a common and very contagious disease among goldfish which results in many deaths. The spores of the fungus, *Saprolegnia*, are often present in ponds and aquaria, but can gain entry to the fish only through wounds.

The spread of the fungus can sometimes be halted by the mercurochrome treatment (p 25), or by the salt treatment. The affected fish should be put into isolation and given a bath in a 3% saline solution for 15–20 minutes daily. Sulphonamide drugs, available on veterinary prescription, may be needed for advanced cases.

Saprolegnia or White Fungus

Constipation

Trailing faeces are an indication of constipation, which often results from feeding goldfish exclusively on dried food. Fresh food (p 20), and particularly green food, a fish tonic and an increase in water temperature should effect a cure.

Icthyopthiriasis or White Spot

Fin rot

Great Diving Beetle

Larva of Great Diving Beetle

White spot disease, *Icthyopthiriasis*
Another common, contagious and often fatal ailment of fish is white spot disease, caused by a parasite and characterized by tiny white spots all over the skin, fins and gills.

Visibly scaled goldfish can be treated by isolating affected fish in a temporary tank for 8–10 days with no water plants, and adding enough methylene blue to turn the water blue-black.

Calico varieties may be treated with a bath made up of 5 drops of 2% mercurochrome solution in 5l/1.1gal of water for 3 hours a day. Mercurochrome is very poisonous, but a 2% solution can be bought from a chemist. The same treatment is recommended for *Saprolegnia* (p 24).

Fin rot
Accidental tears and splits to the fins heal of their own accord, but fin rot is the wasting of the tissue between the fin rays. The salt bath treatment (p 24) is recommended, but fin rot is considered to be the result of poor feeding and inadequate living conditions, and only an improvement in these will bring about a lasting cure.

Swim bladder disease
Loss of balance is the most obvious symptom, although non-specific, of swim bladder disease, which is common among goldfish, and particularly so among the highly bred fancy varieties.

Although there is no known cure for the disease, the condition is sometimes relieved by keeping the affected fish in shallow water for a few days and giving the salt bath treatment (p 24).

Predation
Goldfish fall victim to birds such as the heron, but there are also less obvious predators in a pond. The Great Diving Beetle, *Dytiscus*, and its larvae can kill goldfish.

The Healthy Goldfish

In general goldfish are hardy and healthy, and their distressingly high mortality rate is more often due to poor living conditions, wrong feeding, bad handling, foul water, injury, pest, or sudden temperature fluctuation rather than to disease.

A sick fish should be isolated in a separate tank, and if the cause of its loss of condition has been due to poor living accommodation, this move alone may effect a cure.

A new fish should also be kept in isolation for a period, to ensure that disease is not transmitted to existing stock.

The signs of health in goldfish are as follows:

Abdomen	well-rounded, neither hollow, nor distended, except in females carrying eggs.
Appetite	good in well-oxygenated water on warm days. Appetite much diminished in cold water and warm water low in oxygen.
Breathing	a rhythmical rise and fall of the gill covers indicates normal breathing. Gulping at the surface is a sign of oxygen starvation.
Demeanour	alert to stimuli, active in warm water, although activity much reduced in cold water, or when oxygen is low. Gregarious: one fish leaving the shoal to lurk alone may be in deteriorating health.
Eyes	bright and clear.
Fins	entire, without tears, splits, white spot, or streaks of blood. Fins should be held away from the body. Drooping and folded fins are a symptom of ill-health.
Position in water	freely swimming on an even keel. Sick fish may sink to the bottom, or float on the surface on their side.
Scales	scales should be covered with a mucus, which is a protective body covering while it remains unbroken. Scales should show no injury or fungal growth.
Vent	clean, free of faeces, which do not trail from a healthy fish.

Life History

Scientific name	*Carassius auratus*
Name of young	fry
Eggs hatch	4–14 days
No. of eggs shed	1000–3000
Fertilization	external
Puberty	8–12 months
Adult coloration	8–12 months
Best age to breed	$2\frac{1}{2}$–3 years
Spawning season	April–September
Spawning cycle	monthly
Spawning duration	12 hours (approx.)
Length at 5 years	20cm/8in (Common goldfish)
Adult length	40cm/16in (Common goldfish)
Life expectancy	25 years (Common goldfish) 14 years (Fancy varieties)

Reproduction

Sexing goldfish

Even fish biologists make no claim to being able to sex a goldfish on sight, except those in breeding condition. Then the female will show an abdomen swollen by an ovary full of eggs, which is the hard roe of edible fish, and the male will produce enough sperm, or milt, in the soft roe to fertilize the eggs of many females. The males also have white tubercles on the gill covers at this time, and on the pectoral fins that may look enlarged.

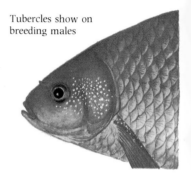

Tubercles show on breeding males

Breeding season

The breeding season begins in April or May and continues throughout the summer. Mature fish over one year old who are in breeding condition are capable of spawning approximately monthly during the season.

Breeding condition

Breeding condition can be encouraged by good feeding in the spring. The goldfish will need a high protein diet with plenty of fresh food, such as water fleas and scraped meat. An increased diet will allow them to produce eggs and milt as well as normal growth. Goldfish will not usually breed in water that is not clean and well oxygenated.

Breeding in a pond

Goldfish have been known to breed in temperatures ranging from 10°–21°C/50°–70°F, but the perfect day for the first spawning is a warm, still day in early summer. A shallow pond margin, where the water will quickly warm through, is ideal and will encourage breeding, as also will the presence of water weeds or bundles of willow twigs which can be put there especially to receive the eggs as they are laid.

Pregnant female viewed from above

Spawning

Spawning behaviour is noisy and unmistakable. The males chase the females through the pond into the

Eggs adhering to pondweed

Dull coloration of immature goldfish

shallows, with much splashing and commotion that causes them to release batches of eggs over any available water plants or substitutes.

The males release milt over the eggs, thereby fertilizing them. Spawning frequently begins early in the morning and may continue all day.

The eggs

The eggs, which are the size of pin heads, and look like clear jelly, float singly through the water in their thousands and, being sticky, adhere to whatever plants they were released over. The eggs and the young fry are in danger of being eaten by adult fish in the pond, and for safety should either be removed, still attached to their support, to a hatching tank or netted off from the main area of water. The warmer water of the shallows, if partitioned off, makes an ideal natural hatchery.

Breeding in an aquarium

Aquarium breeding is more suitable for a pair of fish than for many. It is necessary to have a well-fitting glass partition that can be used for two purposes: first to separate the adults for a few days, so that when it is removed they are encouraged to spawn; and then to separate them from the eggs.

Hatchery tank

A hatching tank may be used for the eggs laid in either pond or aquarium. It should be filled with fresh tap water, and left to stand for a few hours, before introducing the eggs with the plants to which they are attached. A sunny window sill will be a suitable position to maintain the water at 21°C/70°F, but strong sunshine falling directly on the water surface is too intense for the fry. Duckweed may be floated on the surface to provide shade, while the temperature remains high enough to encourage good growth.

The Young

The eggs hatch in 4 to 14 days, according to temperature. Ideally, in a temperature of 21°C/70°F, they will hatch in 4 days; at 10°C/50°F hatching will take 14, and all that time eggs are in danger from water snails, larvae and adult goldfish.

When they first emerge, the young fry look like fine hairs and continue to hang from the plants. In a few days, when they are free-swimming, they will have absorbed their own yolk-sacs and will need a proprietary food specially prepared for fry. Those in a pond will also be able to feed naturally, on microscopic animal life.

In nature, thousands of eggs are laid, but only a few fish reach maturity; in captivity, it may be that too many are being raised in a confined space. It should be remembered that the fish capacity of a tank (p 9) is very limited, and it has been calculated that to rear 1,000 fry to a length of 2.5cm/1in would need eighty-four tanks measuring 60 × 30 × 30cm/24 × 12 × 12in.

At one month, fry can begin to make the transition to adult diet; at three months, hardy breeds may be put out into a pond. These are dull in colour; the full glory of their adult gold may take a year to develop.

A safe nursery area can be made for the fry by partitioning off one end of the pond with a small-mesh net. The shallow pond margin is particularly suitable for the development of the young

Group of young Lionhead

Index